CW00542872

THE BOOK OF NOTHING

A Song of Enlightenment

SOSAN'S HSIN HSIN MING

THE BOOK OF NOTHING

A Song of Enlightenment

SOSAN'S HSIN HSIN MING

Translated by
PHILIP DUNN AND PETER JOURDAN

**Andrews McMeel
Publishing**

Kansas City

Design by Amy Ray

ISBN: 0-7407-2725-7

Library of Congress Control Number on file

Table of Contents

INTRODUCTION

The Book of Nothing, or *Hsin Hsin Ming*, as it was originally titled, was written in China at the end of the sixth century by an enlightened Buddhist monk named Seng T'san or Sosan. Seng T'san was the third patriarch in the emerging tradition of Zen which had its beginnings in China and which flowered in Japan. Sosan is the Japanese translation of the name Seng T'san. Because this ancient monk and his remarkable text are more relevant to the Zen tradition than the Buddhist one, we refer to him as Sosan.

Not much is known of Sosan, but the text he left behind is an inspiration to seekers of every tradition. It succinctly and very simply captures the essence of the empty mind that in the generations to come was to be the hallmark of the Zen tradition.

The empty mind, or no-mind, loosely describes the state in which reality is experienced without being filtered through the thought process of the mind. Without this filter, reality is experienced as completely fresh, radiant, and luminous—and, as if for the first time. Inherent in this experience is a feeling of both joy and bliss.

The state of no-mind is not easily entered into. It may happen from time to time for a moment or two, but to cultivate it as a permanent state is the lifelong work of a very dedicated soul. Sosan was such a soul. He reached the peak of human experience known to us as enlightenment and it is from there he has written this gem.

Hsin Hsin Ming can be loosely interpreted to mean "my song." Like the music that flows through a musician's flute, the experience described by Sosan is a melody that has flowed through a human voice. It is most likely that Sosan spoke these words and that they were written down by those who listened to him. Like the flute player's song, Sosan's *Hsin Hsin Ming* can never truly be sung again.

Nonetheless it has a life of its own. The beauty inherent in these few words lies in the experience they point to. The state of no-mind is a state of silence, of joy and compassion. It is the state in which life can be lived in such contentment that the corrupting desires of the body-mind cease to be a problem. For this reason, Sosan's *Hsin Hsin Ming* or *Book of Nothing* serves as an inspiration that can be read again and again and meditated upon line by line.

THE STORY OF SOSAN AND THE HSIN HSIN MING

Almost one thousand years after the death of Gautama Buddha in India, it happened that Bodhidharma, who was twenty-eighth in a direct lineage from him, had been travelling around the country for many years. Buddhists at that time were being persecuted in India, so Bodhidharma headed north towards China.

When he arrived there, more that eighty thousand Buddhist monks were already living in Chinese temples, creating an atmosphere of great devotion by performing ceremonies, teaching meditation and reciting sutras (scriptures), but not one of these monks made an impact comparable to that of Bodhidharma.

Bodhidharma's approach was a radical departure from that of traditional Buddhism. He did not go to the temples. He did not recite sutras. Instead he wandered about the country as a simple monk and encouraged those who came near to sit in silence. Then, with loud noises and sudden shocks he provoked them to have an immediate experience of what he called no-mind. His methods were simple and direct—and his disciples very few. "Whatever you are doing," Bodhidharma would say, "whether it is walking, sitting, standing, lying down, what you are doing does not matter: Do it silently, without any stirring of thoughts. This is meditation."

This new form of Buddhism that Bodhidharma taught was not appreciated by the mainstream Chinese. They thought him to be wild and uncouth. His methods flew straight in the face of their civilized approach and did not offer the solace they sought. It is not surprising, therefore, that soon after he died, Bodhidharma's disciples began to be persecuted.

Before Bodhidharma's death he had passed his work on to a successor named Hui-k'o who had to flee into the mountains to hide for many years. There, hidden in mountain caves, a few disciples would gather around him, and Hui-k'o continued to nurture the new methods of Bodhidharma. He and his disciples would sit silently gazing at an empty wall—waiting. As they moved slowly about the country they provoked each other with intuitive insights and surprise actions. They forsook the memorization of sutras and the postured attitudes of devotion. A new lightheartedness entered their world. They ceased to be bogged down by the complicated interpretations of Buddhist teachings which had emerged since Buddha's death.

One of the disciples of Hui-k'o was a gentle man named Sosan. He followed Hui-k'o as he fled from mountain cave to mountain cave and was devoted to this new work. After his own enlightenment, Sosan, fearing that the teachings of Bodhidharma would be lost to the world, created the *Gatha*, or song, called *Hsin Hsin Ming*.

Over time, the persecution of the new sect abated and eventually interest in it grew. It was not too long before young monks from Japan were seeking out Masters of these new techniques. From one to another a special transmission happened that was lighthearted and irrational—situations were created that would stop the disciple's mind and in that moment, when their mind was still, they would have a glimpse of reality, naked and true.

From Bodhidharma to Hui-k'o, and on through Sosan and his followers, meditation was taught in a way that had profound results. Meditation, the word for which was *dhyan* in India became *zh'an* or *ch'an* in China. When it reached Japan the word became *zh'an* or Zen.

In later years, when the history of Zen began to be told, Bodhidharma became known as the first patriarch of Zen. Hui-k'o became the second, and Sosan, the third. There is a single short story told of Sosan in the *Denku-roku* or *Account of the Transmission of the Lamp*, by Keizan. It gives us an idea of the manner in which Master Hui-k'o and the young disciple Sosan engaged.

Sosan approached Master Hui-k'o and said to him, "My mind is possessed by thoughts. I beg you, Master, wipe away these thoughts."

Hui-k'o appeared surprised and sent Hui-k'o away saying, "Go. Find your thoughts and bring them to me, then I will wipe them away for you."

Sosan went outside. After some time he returned and said, "Although I've looked for my thoughts, I can't find them."

To this Hui-k'o replied, "It seems then that I have done a good job of wiping away your thoughts."

HSIN HSIN MING

OR

THE BOOK OF NOTHING

by Sosan

The Great Way is effortless
for those who live in choiceless awareness.
To choose without preference
is to be clear.

Even the slightest personal preference
and your whole world becomes divided.
To perceive reality as it is
is to live with an open mind.

When the lens you look through

reflects your personal bias,

your view of reality is clouded.

Truth simply is.

The clouded mind cannot know it.

The Great Way is empty—
like a vast sky.
Silence the busy mind
and know this perfection.

Be seduced neither by the outer world
nor by your inner emptiness.
Reside in the oneness of things
where distinctions are meaningless.

Trying to still the mind

inhibits the experience of oneness,

for the very action of trying

is the busy mind at work.

Live in the Great Way

where action is stillness and silence pervades.

Deny the reality of things
and miss true nature.
Assert that emptiness exists
and it will disappear.

To experience reality,
stop using words;
for the more you talk about things
the farther away from the truth you stray.

Return to oneness and discover its essence.

Being dazzled by appearance

you miss the truth.

Go beyond both appearance and emptiness

and find the unmoving center.

Duality appears in minutest traces;
carefully avoid the trap.
Pursue the confusion of your opinions
and the eternal mind is lost.

Rather than focus on knowing the truth
simply cease to be seduced by your opinions.
If there is even an inkling of right or wrong
the enlightened mind ceases to be.

Everything there is comes from oneness
but oneness cannot be described.
Holding any trace of it in the mind
is to deny the essence of emptiness.

When the mind is still,
nothing can disturb it.
When nothing can disturb it,
reality ceases to exist in the old way.

When you understand the relationship

of subject and object,

thinker and thought—

and how they create each other—

you recognize that these are not two, but one.

Don't strive to know particulars
when what you want to experience is one.
It is beyond the nature of the mind to perceive
the reality it cannot describe.

Oneness has nothing to do with hard or easy

for it is beyond every opposite.

It cannot be found, it cannot be retained.

To grasp at it is to miss it entirely.

Not trying to go faster or slower,

be still,

and let go.

Just let things be

for it is exactly as it should be.

Returning to your true nature,
spontaneity and essence are found.
This is the space that always exists
and that holds all within.

True reality is hidden by the practice of thought
but also in the denial.
Accept the reality of not naming things
and rest in the silence of being.

The need to name, the need to distinguish
are born of a clinging fear.
Remain unattached to every thought
and know the true nature of being.

Use your senses to experience reality,
for they are part of your empty mind.
This empty mind takes note of all it perceives
and is guided by its sensing needs.

While the ignorant are bound to emotional choices—
attaching themselves to their ignorance,
the wise experience life through not reacting at all—
unswayed, uninvolved, unattached.

Be inattentive and mind is an irritant
with dreams that disturb reality.
Why look for trouble and distress
when awareness is so freeing?

High and low, good and bad—
all duality disappears,
and all dreams abate
when the inner calm is met.

When the mind ceases all movement,

ceases judging,

ceases conceptualizing,

the deep cool essence of suchness

becomes a way of life.

When all things are perceived
with an open mind,
they return to their natural way.
Without any movement, without any description,
they are an undivided part of the whole.

True nature is impartial;
it has no causes or rules.
With the mind in undivided unity,
wisdom is radiated.

Trust in true nature,
keep your heart strong.
Pure mind is pure wisdom,
to part from it is foolish.

When there is neither "self" nor "other,"

awareness simply is.

All is empty,

all is clear,

no effort is made for none is needed.

Meet doubt directly
with the words "not two"
and know that nothing can be separate
and all is one.

There is nothing that is not included:
This is an eternal truth.
The very small and the very large are equal,
boundaries and limits do not exist.

Absolute reality is beyond time and space,
being and non-being both exist;
for whether you see it or not
is of no consequence.

Empty and infinite
existing as one,
opening before your eyes,
A vast presence.

One thing is all things, and all things are one.

What is and what is not are equals.

Once this is realized

there is no need to worry about anything.

To live and to trust in the non-dual mind

is to move with true freedom,

to live without anxiety,

upon the Great Way.

Language contains no way to describe

the ultimate unity of suchness:

Beyond belief, beyond expression,

beyond space, beyond time.

ACKNOWLEDGMENTS

Page 5: *An Offering for Long Life to the Holy Maiden*, Anonymous, © National Palace Museum Collection, Republic of China.

Pages 8, 12, 13, 26, 29, 30, 42, 61: © British Museum, London.

Pages 17, 21, 22, 37, 38, 45, 46, 50, 53, 54, 57, 65, 66, 70, 73, 77, 78: © Asian Art Museum, San Francisco.

Page 18: enlarged detail from *Night Rain at Karasaki* by Utagawa Hiroshige, © Ota Memorial Museum, Tokyo.

Page 25: *Pines in the Snow* by Maruyama Okyo, © Mitsui Bunko, Tokyo.

Pages 33, 41, 58, 62, 74: Detail from *A True View of Mount Asama* by Aodo Denzen, © Tokyo National Museum, Tokyo.

Pages 34, 49: *Living Abroad or Returning Home Are After All the Same Thing* by Xian Yuncong, © Rietburg Museum, Zurich.

Page 69: *Flowering Cherries at Yoshinoyama* by Watanabe Shiko, © Private Collection.